Réka Nyitrai is the real deal as a poet.
that take us further into her worlds of   , ------, and 'ghosts
come from duck eggs'. She probes the domestic world to reveal the strange
undercurrents at the heart of family relationships and erotic love. These are
poems that are richly imagistic; and in which anything can become anything
else ('my hands will be reborn as birds') - poems that are transnational,
translingual. Here are echoes of Chinese and Japanese poets; and particularly
of poets such as Joyce Mansour, Chika Sagawa, and Gabriel García Lorca.
But her voice is unique, with its own poetic lexicon, 'the language of slapped
water'. Sparking with dark humour, her work also sings with a gorgeous
lyricism that comes from deep within the Zone of true poetry.
— Liam Carson

Réka Nyitrai is a multilingual force. An international enigma. A surrealist
soothsayer. A spirit who dreams in droplets of water and embers of bone.
Whether writing prose poetry or haiku or (in this case) free verse, her
words extend through the wanderlust of the underworld, the hypothetical
and the magical, the ambient moment before waking. In the four sections
of *Moon Flogged*, clouds talk, a pigeon becomes a hat, phantoms have
ponytails, ants milk cows, and a horse sits in a living room. Husbands
and wives flood the pages, a "rotunda of mothers" casually have cameos,
and family members twirl around like mice. The vocabulary is simplistic
and domestic yet the images are dense and complex, residing inside the
absurdist beyond. Leonora Carrington and Gro Dahle chatter through
these feminist poems, these hymnals, these chants. If Réka blows out
birthday candles, the smoke might be full of crows. See also: wolves. See
also: ghosts. *Moon Flogged* is a tender book of family and loss and grief and
love. It is a menagerie of animals packed with feathers and stuffed with eggs.
— Benjamin Niespodziany

In *Moon Flogged*, Réka Nyitrai mesmerizes with a poetic prowess that
transforms the mundane into the mystical and the familiar into the
otherworldly. With a voice both fierce and delicate, surreal and absurd,
Nyitrai navigates themes of identity, memory, and sexuality, creating a
compelling exploration of the self and the world that is both deeply personal
and universally resonant. Reminiscent of Mary Ruefle, Aase Berg, and Kim
Hyesoon, her poems are a testament to the power of words to capture the
ephemeral and eternal. Here, we have a speaker who is "more beautiful than the
peak of a mountain / seen from a crashing plane." And through her collection,
Nyitrai spectacularly proves her statement: "Poetry is the mother of all cakes."
— Karan Kapoor

MOON FLOGGED

Réka Nyitrai is a Romanian-Hungarian poet who discovered her poetic voice at forty-one, mainly through Japanese short forms, but particularly haiku. Her debut haiku collection *While Dreaming Your Dreams* won the Haiku Society of America Touchstone Distinguished Books Award for 2020. Following this, she began to write both prose and lineated poems. She writes in English, her third language. She is a spell, a sparrow, a lioness's tongue — a bird nest in a pool of dusk.

Also by Réka Nyitrai

While Dreaming Your Dreams   (Mono Ya Mono Books, 2020)

To Alan Peat

ISBN: 978-1-916938-47-2

Cover designed by Aaron Kent

Edited and Typeset by Aaron Kent

Broken Sleep Books Ltd
PO BOX 102
Llandysul
SA44 9BG

CONTENTS

SMALL HOLES BETWEEN THE LIPS

DRAGONS IN A TINY BOX

MOON FLOGGED

GODDESS OF HUNT AND CHASTITY

Moon Flogged

Réka Nyitrai

Broken Sleep Books

SMALL HOLES
BETWEEN THE LIPS

FUNK

The woman wearing a mask of roses is carrying a pork chop.
The dogs the clouds walk are howling ladybirds.
That's all folks for the pigeons to peck.
They are all objects of adoration — says a visitor.
While the clouds are moving like future automobiles
bold and reckless, the pork chop stinks and feels ashamed.
The woman wearing a veil of roses
gives up her son for adoption.
Wait, says a ladybird, *wait* says a cloud,
but the pictures are done and the woman has gone.
What lingers is the pork chop's stench.

TURNTABLE

Robin song filled with cake rusk

In a woodpecker's nest a school of poets filing paid bills to deter snakes

Six glossy white eggs to last the whole voyage

Imminent hatchlings and a small hole between the lips

The goal is to be self-made like the private language of soft rocks

With a pinch of salt another mandala

Beautiful rain seeder

You make me love you

Halfway bold, halfway apple

Between the neck and breast of a bird

If only I hadn't become a needle

CAKES

The cake is a bonus. The wind brings whispers
uttered by ancestors. One of the guests
is an ocelot. He is the one who brought the cake.
He is a wealthy business man. One of his many companies
produces and sells sewing needles and crochet hooks.
I am sitting on the floor surrounded by imaginary
gifts. My long, long giraffe-neck touches a cloud.
From here I see clearly — poetry is the mother of all cakes.

TENDERFOOT

Dreaming of one day being a white tigress.
As fearless as a cloud.
As aggressive and uncontrollable
as a cricket's chirp.
Until then I sharpen my claws
counting syllables for a haiku.

LANDSCAPE WITH NO HAT

I leave the house without an umbrella
and notice that it's raining. I grab a pigeon
and start wearing it as a hat. A man sheltered
under the shop's eaves compliments my look.
Let's paint a picture of your hat – he says
and we do. But in the painting, there is no hat or pigeon,
only a nude woman giving birth to the moon.

PUNK KARMA

Until I do not feast on
one hundred *little slices of death*,
father, you will not be
reborn!

MEMORY

Like a spider
of past evenings
I saw you
Gala Dalí
descending
from a rose stalk.
Your soft, small body
wore nothing but a window.
Through you I could see
the reflections of
lost sunsets & a gull
pecking at my lips.

RAIN-MAKER'S TO-DO LIST

- Pull out a blue snake from a closed umbrella
- Herd the clouds into a bird that never flew
- Harvest the dreams of seven weeks spent alone, under a tree
- Sweep the ants back into the ghost's ponytail
- Make a spell on a tulip carved on a gravestone
- Take the salt out of a kiss

WILD FLOWERS

This morning
I tried to count
the bees that live inside my head.
I tried to figure out
why I feel loneliest
surrounded by people.
Then, I imagined
being a ghost,
carrying flowers
to the graves of my loved ones.
Flowers with puckered lips.
Flowers with teeth.
Flowers that bite off the shadows' nose,
and roam the fields
collecting bones.

MOON LANDING

Where is my lover?
My lover is inside a conch shell.

Who is my lover?
My lover is Buddha's tiny umbrella.

What is the function of a tiny umbrella?
Little girls use it to protect them from ghosts.

Where do ghosts come from?
Ghosts come from duck eggs.

What is an egg?
An egg is the double of the moon.

Can bad girls like me reach the moon?
Yes, they can. With their pinky toes.
If their eyes are firmly closed.

FIRST WORDS

Not in the language I write in today,
neither in the language I use to tell my lover how much I want him,
but rather, in the language of slapped water;
the language of wing-rubbed clouds;
a humming, a whistling
carried to the swans, my twin sisters,
saying this —
I am reborn.

PORTRAIT OF MY DESIRES AS A NAPKIN

I spread out a cloud
on your nightstand.
Maybe later,
while you sleep,
I will scribble a poem on it.

DRAGONS IN A TINY BOX

MEN CANNOT MULTITASK

On Monday I sing to make the grass grow.
On Tuesday I wear polka dots
and help ants milk their cows.
On Wednesday I teach clouds to rhyme.
On Thursday I read bedtime stories
to two dragons sleeping in a tiny box.
On Friday I knit mittens for lonely Bugs Bunnies.
On Saturday and Sunday, I am a fox cub
feasting on dandelions.

TWIN STRANGERS

Sitting next to me on the train there is a beautiful woman.
Glancing at her mink coat and pearl earrings I cannot imagine her
        any other way,
but happy and rich. As if reading my mind, she starts to tell me
        how happy she is,
living with her husband and their lovely daughter in a big house
        with a
roof made of cakes. Before dozing off, she kindly asks me
to remind her to disembark at a station called Crossroads.
While she is sleeping, head resting on my arm,
legions of crabs flee from her heart.

THE 12TH HOUSE

I broke my father's terracotta pillow.
I broke it with the heel of my shoe.
He cursed me to be beautiful.
He cursed me to be red.

I have learned that
in every unfinished dream
there is a south-facing window.
I have also learned to beg.
For this reason only,
I will return
to die by your hand.

The gerberas must first be positioned
in full light.

NOT CONTAGIOUS

I am
meant to be played with
not left in the dark
beheaded
imagining kindness
and waiting for a kind soul to take me
to the doll hospital.

A voice once told me
bad girls aren't born, but made.

My mother's spells don't work.
My husband's plea doesn't work.
I put on my pink shorts
and leave this house.

SUMMER INTO FALL

I see myself as a wolf growing its thick, warm coat.
If I have to choose between summer and fall, I choose fall
the season of new, kinkier loves.
All summer, my husband and I were saving money — home cooking.
We made traditional eggplant spread and served it cold,
with bread, tomatoes, and cheese.
All summer, I exchanged blue letters with real and not so real friends.
To prevent me from screaming, all summer, I wore a mask of thistles.
Yes, fall is the season I love the most for I can lie down between
   yellowed leaves,
curl my tail over my snout and catch my warm breath.
This is what I call quality time alone.
This is what you call self-love.
After so many years, I might even say that I am ready
to leave this den and start a new pack.

ASTRONAUT TRAINING

As soon as housewives begin baking moon-cakes
they start to behave like movie stars.
They stop doing the dishes and do not mend
their husband's socks. They spend more and more time
in front of the mirror, dreaming of remodeled bodies.
They do not care if supper burns.
They grow their nails long and paint them red.
At solstice you can see them digging holes in the backyard,
hiding the money, they have saved for their Princess Adventures.

NOT CALLED PEGASUS

This year we are keeping a horse in the living room.
Needless to say, all our guests want to sit on it.
But our horse does not want to be ridden.
He has higher goals than being used and controlled.
Mainly, he spends his days learning
to fly by watching documentaries on YouTube.
He considers this stage of his life
an intermediate stage
and looks forward to the day
he will become winged and take flight.
Being proactive, he already sent his name
to Mars.

POEM BEGINNING WITH A LINE BY MARK LEIDNER

On a planet where people have no mouths
there's no such thing as hunger or thirst.
People live happily, absorbing sunshine and rainwater through
their skin.
The only time they are a little sad is
when they want to declare their love to someone
but, having no mouths, they can't speak.
They express their love by drawing cotton candy clouds
on the water's surface
with a pen and blue ink.
They kiss by rubbing their nose
against their partner's cheek.

HAPPY BIRTHDAY

Other women's husbands are perfect
in their imperfection. They call their wives darling,
give them flowers and pull the chair out
for them. Once, in an elegant restaurant,
I saw a man kneeling at his wife's feet
while massaging her soles.
I wanted to tell him
he is my hero. I think that was the summer
when you lived in Bucharest and I lived in Budapest
and you texted me every day
and told me that you would like me to be your tiny bird;
a bird you would shelter in the sunniest corner of your heart.
After twenty years of marriage
I'm still waiting for you
to surprise me with a bouquet of flowers
on my birthday.

WOMAN DRESSED IN BLACK

I believe my hands will be reborn as birds.

Probably as sparrows or pigeons,
depending on their and god's mood.

From the balcony of an old gothic house
a woman dressed in black will throw them seeds.

For now, my hands are doing what they love to do:
with red feathers they are caressing the nape of my lover's neck.

I love my hands. I hate my hands—
says the woman dressed in black.

I'LL CALL THOSE THINGS NOT SCARY

A cento

All night I waited for you to saw off my head.

You'd think I'd be scared
but I'm not scared.

You inspire me.

I found a dead body in the pond.
I rise up out of the pond.

A girl falls asleep thinking,
"forever, forever, forever"
father raised children
to eat them.

I'm
looking for the girl.
Like a snail she crawls under a huge
rock.

When you
open the door
I'm in labour
delivering death.

*with lines from Lesle Lewis,
Zachary Schomburg and Kim Hyesoon

THE BURIAL

A cento

There are two black men holding hammers.
From the bottomless pit they lop off the neck of night.
Trains crawl along the bulging street,
incessantly obstructing
the sleep of figs.
Flinging inwards,
I discover a newly drowned body.
So please, now tell me,
who blindfolds me from behind
as if spreading white linen
as if laughing
as if to say "yes",
while gradually hardening into a
mound?

with lines from Chika Sagawa, Ayane Kawata,
Sumiko Yagawa, Kyong-Mi Park

A LULL

A cento

You crawled after the rain
and lapped up the boils on the earth's crust.
Blindly in love
got it all backwards.
Hurry, I thought, and my hands were like birds
reflected as a white tree
in brown water.
"Oh," I said, or my love said to me
"It is hard to die without writing poems..."
Legs, dirtied green,
run!

*with lines from Vasko Popa, Chika Sagawa, John Sakkis, Cecilia Woloch, Chelsey Minnis

HARDNESS

For my birthday I asked the devil to give me
a pair of silver boots. But he grew angry,
slapped me and called me a whore.
When he cooled down,
he treated me to bonbons and champagne.
He even prepared a foamy bubble bath
and read me a poem entitled "White",
all the while, tracing with his fingertips,
the milk that oozed from my hard
stone breasts.

MOON FLOGGED

TANKA

Tied to a stone table
with a bird in my mouth
I watch how the moon flogs me
with a whip
braided from my locks.

THERAPY

After my mother
gave birth to my brother
she did not let my father
have sex with her any more.
Instead, she preferred
to have her belly caressed with
a peacock's feather.
I still remember
how she used to laugh
and laugh...
and then cry.

THE BLUE APRON

My brother
hates everything
that does not taste
of his mother's milk.
Be it plum brandy, Coca Cola,
or a woman's most intimate parts —
all are undesirable.
With a fine education
he has no life but the one he lives
in front of the TV grazing on sandwiches.
Tied to his mother's apron strings
he is that horse whose blue neigh
bathes me in cold sweat.
I'm wondering if I'll ever be able
to feed him milk.

ZOOEROTICA

The first time I meet K I walk into his bedroom,
tie my blue horse to his bed pole and leave it to graze on the ghosts
of his former lovers. They are legion and all quite different.
The sudden neigh of my gorging horse makes me wet.
Before copulating, I ask him to read some poems.
He puts on his eyeglasses and he reads, what else,
if not a Bukowski poem! All day long, as wolves and foxes
eat my heart from his hands, I let him pet the creatures inside me.

QUESTIONS I ASK MY HUSBAND WHILE PONDERING BREAK-UP

How long do butterflies live in captivity?
Do birds kiss? And if they do, how often?
What is the color of loneliness?
Is loneliness a disease?
Can a cheat still love the person they cheated on?
Are freckles considered beautiful?
What name means moon in Japanese?
What sins will keep us out of heaven?
Will you learn all my poems by heart, if I die?

POEM EXCLUDING SPRING

after Noah Falck

I wash your feet
until you become a cathedral.
At night I dream of daffodils
and recall that June is the luckiest month
to marry. I try to remember whose poem
it is that juxtaposes a winter strawberry
and a wedding dress.
I am beautiful, but lonely.
Many times, I wake up and find myself
at our wedding, dancing. The mother of the bride
is not my mother.

FOREVER YOUNG

I am beautiful.
As beautiful as a winter fountain or a cloud.
I'm hopeless. Just like my mother's attempt
to quench the devils' thirst by serving them
red melon sprinkled with salt.
I don't want to grow old. I want to play.
I want to eat melon and strawberry every day.
I am more beautiful than the peak of a mountain
seen from a crashing plane.
I am beautiful and vain.
I am a burning pilot fallen on your tablecloth.

HANDS

I went to the palmist and found out
that perched on my life line there is a sparrow,
or maybe a star.
The hand is our most useful tool, but from all parts
of the body, hands are the first
to wither and they are most prone
to get injured— said the palm reader.
This made me recall my grandmother;
how she always slapped my hand when I did something wrong.
I never wept but all my anger gathered in my hands
and I started to see them as ugly.
Then I remembered the first time I received a compliment:
You have youthful hands. They are beautiful. —
said the manicurist and I, like a fool, could not stop crying.
Why is it that a sparrow, or maybe a star perched on my lifeline? —
I wanted to ask the palmist, but in the room
there was no-one around me, only darkness.
I bowed my head and started to pet and kiss my
beautiful ugly hands.

CARNATIONS

When my father died
he took away my face.
I think he did so
because he had no recent
pictures of me.
Anyway, from that moment on
where once I had my face
I now have a garden
of red carnations.

TABLE

broadside
to the wind
a rotunda of mothers
carved of
the hipbone
of Noah's
oldest son

MEMORIES

In the poultry yard
the little girl talks to the hens.
She tries to describe
the cut and shape
of her future wedding dress.
In the kitchen grandmother
stirs the polenta.
In the backyard grandfather
milks the foxes and wolves
that want to steal grandmother's
chickens.
He dips his moustache in their red milk
and draws hearts
on the little girl's
white cheeks.
No one enters this house
without becoming sad.

DIAPAUSE

This is the bait
birders use
to entice skylarks
to perch on
their eyelids —
said my lover
and handed me
the burlap sack of his heart.
What do you feed a baby bird? —
I wanted to ask him
but it was already winter
and I was hiding in the corner
of an abandoned house.

DEAR MARTIANS,

I live on the 29th floor of a high-rise.
Mostly I awake to the sound of my alarm clock
or the noises the neighbors above make.
They either have rough sex, slam a door or flush the toilet.
Still heavy-eyed, I make tea for my hubby, coffee for myself and for
        both of us sandwiches.
Between chores, I check the weather and speed-read some poems.
Fact-checkers, check: am I happy or sad?
I would say, most often, I swing between happy and sad
just like the old trapeze artist swings between
fear and acceptance whilst awaiting the day he will be laid off.
Anyway, who's going to the circus these days,
when from your window you can see
beautiful people falling through the air?
Sometimes, when I wave at them, they respond.
They mostly give me the finger.
For teaching me what courage means
I reward them with tears.

STILL LIFE WITH ANGELS

this angel has no small change
she wears Prada
and awaits a cab

this angel with flowing blonde hair
could easily be mistaken for the President's assistant

this angel with paper wings
looks like someone who might have read the complete works of
Plato

she just wants me to know
that to escape somewhere new and wonderful
her therapist advised her to read poetry every day

while she is awaiting her cab
she treats me to the latest lines she has memorized
from Emily Dickinson

if you want to see more angels, she says,
tomorrow, in the early morning
you may see them queuing for coffee
at Starbucks.

GODDESS OF HUNT
AND CHASTITY

POEM EXCLUDING PALMISTRY

after Noah Falck

A monarch butterfly lays its eggs
inside your dimples. This is your dream.
Outside, a conspiracy of ravens
takes over the puppet show. Blindfolded, gagged,
suspended between the branches of a tree
I always knew that the hand that so wonderfully fills
my body is the hand god sent
to write on my walls: kissing is the new death.

DECEMBER

In Sweden a man whispers my name
and wants to lie down with me in a field of tulips.
But in Sweden it's mostly winter
and they don't really have tulip fields.
The man has a fever and thinks
snowflakes bleed loneliness.
For weeks he dreams he is a reindeer
and I am the goddess of both the hunt and chastity.
When you love a person, you want them
to leave you, so that you can dream of them...
wrote Max Voloshin to Marina Tsvetaeva.
I agree —
trapped in that man's dream
I want to wake
long before the bullet I shoot
at the reindeer
returns to me.

SELF-PORTRAIT AS SPARROWS

I remember my face:
a cage with a sparrow in it.

I still see the sparrow's brown throat and dun beak —
how it pecks and pecks
at the hand that brings grains of sugar.

During long winter nights,
when I feel the coldest and loneliest,
I knit snow gloves for that hand.

Around my grave sparrows chatter in the bushes
but only one speaks with my mother's voice.

She mainly asks me to interpret her dreams.

SLEEPER

The Tulip Whisperer: do bees speak
the language of rain?
Yes, but they don't like it.
They learned it out of necessity.

Is slowdown actually death?
As long as you use the sun as your compass
sitting still is sleep,
not death.

The Tulip Whisperer: what is the sleep pattern
of bees?
Younger bees sleep much less than the older bees.

Then, regardless of what you say:
sleep is death.

I TRY TO UNDERSTAND HOW POEMS ARE MADE

after Mary Ruefle

Some woodpecker species
peck tree cavities that are perfect circles,
others make oval or oblong nests.
Once, I saw one, in the middle of the city,
expertly hitting its head against a tree.
I felt desperate and strange.
That's when I realized that
I am nothing but a minor poet.
Since then, all I want is
to hit my head against
a passing cloud.

MADE OF OWL'S FEATHERS

Again, I dream
of the golden hook.
It gleams
and cuts the black scent of silence
into small cubes.
I am tired.
This time, I know that
I will not wake up.
Yet, you shall
look for me
even if I do not
believe that you or I
ever existed in any other form
than moon dust.

SELF-PORTRAIT WITH COUNTESS ELIZABETH BÁTHORY DE ECSED

I wear my sunglasses
and my feet are dressed in red high heels.

I can see myself in the lit windows of the shops.
Without being arrogant,
I can assure you that I look flamboyant.

I am asleep yet vigilant.
I pass the drunks, the pimps, the whores,
the homeless and the stray dogs.

It is always like this:
from under my sunglasses I prey on single, good looking men
the ones who look like Johnny Depp or Luca Argentero.

When I glimpse one who is young and beautiful
I grab him by the ear
and shove him in my bag.

When I have three or four of them
I hail a taxi and go home.

At home I undress them
and command them to move on all fours.
For three days and three nights
we play pony play.

Rumor says that
I drink the men's blood.
But this is not true
as I never drink anything,
except shipwrecked champagne.

SELF-PORTRAIT WITH MY FATHER

I wore black clothes for three days.
Then, I learnt that in medieval France
bereaved children wore white.
I paired my white blouses with red pants.
I began a dream journal and invented dreams,
mostly about you and different prehistoric animals:
mastodons, giant sloths and saber-toothed cats.
I did not eat meat and refrained from sex.
For a while, I stopped lying to others and myself.
For a while, my wish to change my life seemed achievable.
Then, I uncovered the mirror and demanding truth I asked this of your
        soul —
Yes or no: when you conceived me, were you quite drunk?

FAREWELL

after Federico Garcia Lorca

If I die,
throw my manuscripts
of gnawed bones
to the dogs.

Watch them bark at my useless metaphors.

If peeing on my self-portraits
would please the dogs,
let them pee.

Take home the fiercest bitch
and dress her in my nightgown.
Before you sleep
beg her to bite off your hand.

I will have my excuse
to come back
and lick up your blood.

(Does anyone know
if devils treat their slaves
to champagne?)

ACKNOWLEDGMENTS

Endless thanks to Alan Peat for his time spent engaging with this work.

Many thanks also to the editors of the following journals who published earlier versions of some of these poems for the first time: *Expat Press; Stone of Madness Press; Action Fokus, the blog of Action Books; The Rusty Truck; weird laburnum; Mercurius; Rat World; Die Leere Mitte; ONLY POEMS; Otoliths; Tint Journal; Twenty-two Twenty-eight; Lost Pilots Lit; Atlas & Alice Literary Magazine.*

LAY OUT YOUR UNREST